# HEALTH CARE
# REFORM

Essential Viewpoints

# HEALTH CARE
# REFORM

## BY LILLIAN E. FORMAN

**Content Consultant**
William Cass McCaughrin, PhD, MPH, Associate Professor
Graduate Department of Health Care Administration,
Trinity University, San Antonio, Texas

# ABDO
Publishing Company

# CREDITS

Published by ABDO Publishing Company, 8000 West 78th Street,
Edina, Minnesota 55439. Copyright © 2010 by Abdo Consulting
Group, Inc. International copyrights reserved in all countries. No
part of this book may be reproduced in any form without written
permission from the publisher. The Essential Library™ is a
trademark and logo of ABDO Publishing Company.

Printed in the United States.

Editors: Erika Wittekind, Mari Kesselring
Copy Editor: Paula Lewis
Interior Design and Production: Nicole Brecke
Cover Design: Nicole Brecke

**Library of Congress Cataloging-in-Publication Data**
Forman, Lillian E.
  Health care reform / by Lillian E. Forman.
     p. cm. — (Essential viewpoints)
  Includes bibliographical references and index.
  ISBN 978-1-60453-532-7
  1. Health care reform—United States—Juvenile literature. I.
Title.

RA395.A3F65 2009
362.1'0425—dc22

                                        2008034907

# TABLE OF CONTENTS

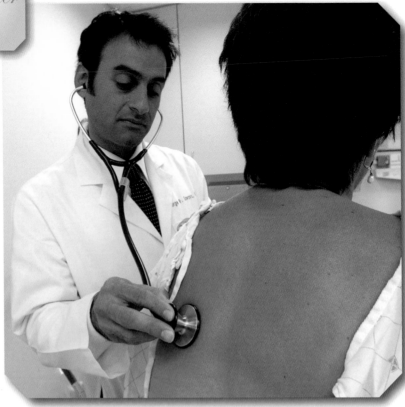

*Dr. George Sawaya examines a patient at the UCSF Women's Health Center in 2006 in San Francisco, California.*

# EVALUATING THE U.S. HEALTH CARE SYSTEM

Almost everyone agrees that the U.S. health care system needs to be changed. What people do not agree on is how. Would a change to a national, or single-payer, system solve the problems? Is total privatization a better answer?

Or is the solution a mixture of the two? How should health care be financed?

In a single-payer system, the federal or state governments would fund the program with money from public taxes. This is sometimes called a national or socialized system. In this system people receive national (or public) health insurance. By contrast, individuals or employers buying policies from insurance companies pay for private health insurance. This is a private health care system. In a universal health care system, everyone within a certain political area, such as a state or a country, is covered. It can be financed privately, nationally, or both. In the United States, the current health care system is a hybrid. This means that it is financed both by private and public (national) sources.

Karen Davenport, author of *Covering America: The U.S. Health Care System and the 2008 Election*, explains why the U.S. system is a hybrid. In 2007, approximately 53 percent of U.S. citizens were covered by private insurance policies provided by their employers. Public insurance programs covered 26 percent of the U.S. population. These programs included Medicare for the elderly, Medicaid for the impoverished, and the State Children's Health Insurance Program

for children under 19. Another 5 percent of the
population bought their own insurance policies.
Approximately 16 percent of the population—nearly
47 million citizens—had no insurance at all.

Medicaid and Medicare are not entirely
dependent on public funds. Medicaid uses private
insurance plans to organize networks, pay claims,
and manage program costs. Medicare recipients can
choose to enroll in private health plans, for which
Medicare pays the premiums. Private insurance
companies manage all of Medicare's drug programs.

## Problems of the U.S. Health Care System

In the first decade of the twenty-first century, the
U.S. health care system faced a number of problems
that reduced its effectiveness. Among these was a
sharp increase in health care spending. In 2007,
total health care costs rose to $2.3 trillion—more
than $7,000 per person. That is an estimated
7 percent increase over the previous year, twice the
rate of inflation. Total U.S. health costs are expected
to increase to $3 trillion by 2011.

The recent increase in expenditures reflects the
rising costs for prescription drugs and inpatient
hospital care. It also is driven by the increase in

use of health care services by people with chronic conditions, such as obesity and heart disease. Additionally, U.S. citizens are simply living longer. This means that a larger percentage of the nation's population will be subject to the ills of old age, which are more chronic and more costly than those of youth. The cost of long-term care facilities and the salaries of their staffs comprise the greatest expenses for Medicare and Medicaid.

Another factor in the continuing rise of U.S. health care costs is the increase in the number of

### Sicko

During the summer of 2007, moviegoers flocked to see *Sicko*. Michael Moore directed and starred in the documentary. The movie began with interviews of people whose insurance companies had denied coverage for them or their relatives. Others who were interviewed had been refused treatment for illnesses they contracted while doing rescue work after the terrorist attacks of September 11, 2001. Moore also showed a clip of an insurance company official who acknowledged refusing treatment to patients to increase her company's profits. Later in the movie, Moore spoke to people from Canada, the United Kingdom, Cuba, and France. Their accounts of their countries' health care systems contrasted sharply with the accounts given by those in the United States.

Reaction to the movie varied widely. Film critic Eric D. Snyder pointed out that Moore dismisses complaints against universal health care systems in other countries by using anecdotes from only a few people. Some of these complaints are that Canadians have to wait a long time for necessary treatment, the French pay exorbitant taxes to support their health care system, and English doctors working for the national program receive smaller salaries than private doctors.

## Capitalism and Health Care

Investment broker John Mugarian is against a capitalistic health care system: "The quality of health care in the United States has deteriorated under for-profit, managed care, and treatments should not be designed based on a corporation's quest to save money. While saving money may make a company's stock go up, denying health care to the sick is immoral. In the past, corporations were able to buy politicians and control the public through the media to keep a publicly sponsored health care system from being implemented. I for one am ready for this to change."[1]

uninsured people. Uninsured people tend to put off seeking medical help. When they finally do go to a doctor, their conditions often have become more serious and, therefore, more expensive to treat. The uninsured also are more likely than the insured to go to emergency rooms, which are legally bound to assess their cases. People without health insurance pay approximately 35 percent of their own medical expenses. Hospitals increase prices to make up the difference. This causes insurance premiums to go up as well. For this reason, those who do have insurance end up paying for the majority of care for those who do not.

High health care expenses have serious consequences for the private citizen and the nation as a whole. In the early 2000s, more and more individuals found that they were unable to pay their medical bills and declared bankruptcy. Nearly half the personal bankruptcies of that period were due to the cost of health care. Among those who had no coverage, an estimated 18,000 people per year died of untreated illnesses.

Employees often receive health care benefits instead of pay raises. They find that their income does not keep up with inflation. This hurts the economy by decreasing their buying power. Business owners that provide health insurance policies for their workers frequently find that the costs of these plans interfere with their ability to invest in new projects. They cannot hire new workers and often have to reduce the existing staff. The decline of businesses and the increase of unemployed people negatively affect the U.S. economy. Tax revenues go down, while demands on social services increase.

## The Heart of the Controversy

Should the solution to these problems be increased government involvement in the U.S. health care system or greater privatization? Proponents of a universal health care system view adequate medical care as a human right. They do not believe

"The fortunate few can afford the latest in medical technology and the most effective new medications, but millions of our fellow citizens are denied today's breakthrough miracle cures. One in six citizens lacks health insurance coverage, and millions more are underinsured. . . . Millions of patients around the nation look to Congress for help in receiving the health care that will save or improve their lives, and we owe them that help."[2]
—*Senator Edward Kennedy*

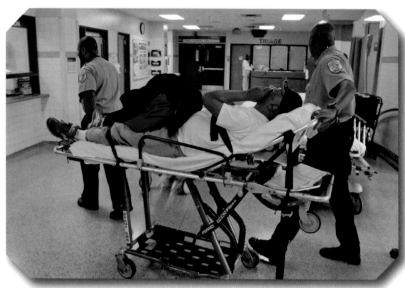

*Paramedics wheel a man into the emergency room at
Grady Memorial Hospital, an Atlanta hospital known for treating the poor.*

that people who can afford private insurance should
receive better medical care than those who cannot.
They say a national, or socialized, health care
program would be less expensive and more efficient.
Such a system would lead to more investment in
long-term care facilities, preventative care, and
better management of chronic conditions. Overall,
the nation's health would be improved. According to
its proponents, this improvement would ultimately
lower health care costs.

Some proponents of universal health care blame conservative political groups, powerful organizations such as the American Medical Association, and private insurance companies for preventing such a system. They accuse these groups of acting to further their own interests rather than the well-being of the American people.

Opponents of universal health care counter by saying that the U.S. health care system is the most innovative and progressive in the world. They argue that publicly funded Medicare and Medicaid have caused the system's problems. An expanded national health care program would have similar financial difficulties and inefficiencies. Running it would require a huge bureaucracy with many salaried employees. They also warn that adopting a national health care system would place the United States on the road to socialism.

Those who do not support a universal health care system may not see health care as a human right. If they do, they may think that a national system does not necessarily guarantee everyone equal access to medical help. Opponents also see some unintended consequences. Without a profit motive, medical researchers might not develop new technology and

"To build a future of quality health care, we must trust patients and doctors to make medical decisions and empower them with better informa-tion and better options. We share a common goal: making health care more affordable and accessible for all Americans. The best way to achieve that goal is by expanding consumer choice, not government control."[3]

—*George W. Bush*

cures. And if citizens did not have to pay for their own medical care, they might not have the incentive to give up or change unhealthy habits.

Almost everyone would agree that the current system has flaws. Many ways to reform U.S. health care have been proposed over the years. Still, disagreement persists on the best solutions to the system's problems.

New Jersey State Senator Joseph Vitale speaks in 2008 about a plan
to cover all state residents with health insurance by 2011.

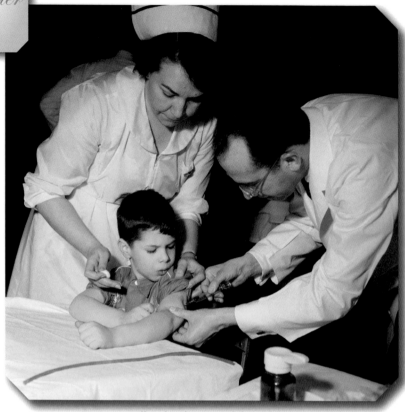

Dr. Jonas Salk, who discovered the polio vaccine,
vaccinates a child in 1964.

# Overview of U.S. Health Care Reform

Receiving effective health care has always been an issue. For many centuries, medical knowledge and technology were extremely limited. Most people, no matter how rich they were, died from infections from injuries or diseases that today can be cured. Even childbirth often ended in death because doctors did not understand the causes of and remedies for infection.

During the twentieth century, medical science advanced. Researchers developed antibiotics that heal severe infections and vaccines that immunize people against diseases. Surgeons learned how to replace damaged organs with healthy or artificial ones.

## HISTORICAL ACCESS TO MEDICAL CARE

Not all U.S. citizens could benefit from these advances, however. While medical technology improved, medical care became more expensive. The system that delivered health care became more exclusive. Nineteenth-century records show that public hospitals in major U.S. cities, such as New York, cared for the rich and poor alike. Public hospitals were not expected to make profits. Patients paid what they could afford. Paying patients, charities, and group health programs supported by employers, unions, and other community organizations kept health care centers functioning.

During the mid-nineteenth century, medical researchers discovered ether, morphine, and chloroform. Since these anesthetics kept patients from struggling, surgical operations were more successful. In the 1880s, a successful treatment was found for rabies. Chances improved for making solid profits from effective services. The medical profession came to be considered more as a business than as a vocation chosen for idealistic reasons. Nonetheless, the seeds of today's problems were taking root, especially toward the end of the nineteenth century. Hospital officials began to investigate charity cases for fraudulent claims. Paying patients received special treatment.

### Early Ideas on Reform

In the early 1900s social reformers pointed out that poverty and illness formed a vicious circle. Poverty caused poor health, and poor health kept people in poverty. Consequently, reformers began to push for legislation that would compel employers to pay their workers a "living wage." The goal was to provide workers with enough income to maintain good health. Healthy workers would be more productive workers. Labor union leaders joined in this campaign.

Some reformers, however, felt it would be too difficult to convince Congress to pass a law requiring employers to raise wages enough to cover the cost of health care. They looked for other solutions and adopted the idea of public health insurance from European social reformers. In 1912, the American Association of Labor Legislation took up this cause. By 1916, the organization's Committee on Social Insurance had drawn up a bill for health insurance to be supported by state taxes.

In addition to helping the disadvantaged, committee members wanted

### Accessible but Inadequate

Sandra Opdycke wrote about the history of New York City hospitals in *No One Was Turned Away*, published in 1999. Opdycke points out that public hospitals in the late 1800s did little to cure their patients:

*The care provided by New York hospitals before the twentieth century served a valuable social function, but it was barely medical in character. During this period a doctor could do little for a patient in a hospital that could not be done as efficiently and often more comfortably elsewhere. Even anesthesia was so rudimentary that it could be provided in a brownstone parlor as well as in a hospital operating room. Moreover, since antisepsis was not widely practiced until late in the nineteenth century, care in a hospital—particularly surgery—often involved higher risks of infection than well-managed home care. When New York Hospital moved to its new building in 1877, its proudest boast was that in the new facility surgery would be "as safe as in the most luxurious home." In general, sick New Yorkers entered a hospital during this period expecting to find not expert medical treatment but care and sustenance.[1]*

to encourage workers to be more productive. They also wanted to reduce administrative difficulties for state governments. Therefore, they created a bill that covered workers who had stable jobs. The bill left out the unemployed, part-time workers, agricultural and domestic workers, and those making more than $100 per month. This meant that underemployed people, such as women, the elderly, disadvantaged minorities, and the disabled, remained without health coverage. Still, this plan was more inclusive than other insurance plans of the time. It provided a model for later attempts to establish a universal health care system.

However, the plan never became law. Physicians feared it would weaken their control over their practices and decrease their incomes. Private insurance companies objected to government interference with their businesses. The American Medical Association also stated that the government should not intrude on the medical profession. The union leaders believed that only by making it possible for workers to buy their own private insurance policies could workers be ensured dignity and equality.

## THE IDEA OF UNIVERSAL HEALTH CARE TAKES HOLD

Although the American Association of Labor Legislation's plan did not succeed, it sparked new ideas about reforming the U.S. health care system. Labor union leaders opposed public health insurance for poor workers on the grounds that it would greatly strengthen class divisions in the United States. Some reformers agreed and began to formulate the idea of universal health coverage.

**Tuberculosis**

During the Great Depression many people suffered from diseases because they lacked the money to seek medical care. One deadly disease during this time was tuberculosis. Tuberculosis is an infection that usually starts in the lungs and spreads to other organs. Common symptoms of tuberculosis are weakness, coughing, chest pain, and shortness of breath. In 1930 tuberculosis resulted in death more than any other contagious disease.

The Great Depression that began in 1929 plunged large numbers of U.S. citizens into poverty. More and more people knew what it was like to be underfed, insufficiently housed, and poorly clothed. When these conditions made them ill, they learned what it was like to lack medical care. The idea of socialized health care gained popularity. Even labor union leaders began to support the idea. President Franklin D. Roosevelt tried to include public health insurance in his 1935 Social Security Act. But the American Medical Association blocked it.

*With former President Harry S. Truman at his side, President Lyndon B. Johnson signs the Medicare bill into law on July 30, 1965.*

During his term of presidency from 1945 to 1953, Harry Truman tried to persuade Congress to set up mandatory health insurance funded by payroll deductions. The American Medical Association fought this plan as well. Conservative political groups also worked against it. They felt that government-sponsored health care would lead to socialism. These groups feared that a socialistic government would interfere with the freedom and independence of the nation's businesspeople.

Gradually, however, more U.S. citizens began to favor the idea of socialized health care. Lyndon B. Johnson was president from 1963 to 1969. In his vigorous war against poverty and other social problems, Johnson worked toward providing national health care. On July 30, 1965, Johnson signed two of his programs—Medicare and Medicaid—into law. Medicare provides health care for the elderly using taxes on individual income. A portion of everyone's paycheck goes toward funding Medicare. Medicaid is a health insurance program for the poor that is supported by funds from both the federal and state governments.

## Reform Attempts in the 1960s and 1970s

Encouraged by the success of Medicare and Medicaid, reformers began to ask for more comprehensive programs. In 1969, during President Richard Nixon's administration, conditions seemed favorable for

**"The Real Daddy of Medicare"**

President Harry Truman's health plan inspired President Lyndon Johnson's Medicare program. When Johnson signed the program into law, Truman joined him. Johnson enrolled Truman into Medicare as its first member. "They told me, President Truman," Johnson said, "that if you wish to get the voluntary medical insurance you will have to sign this application form. . . . So you're getting special treatment since cards won't go out to the other folks until the end of this month. But we wanted you to know, and we wanted the whole world to know, who is the real daddy of Medicare."[2]

**Benefits**

Medicare and Medicaid significantly changed the structure of health care in the United States. The services provided by doctors and hospitals to the elderly and impoverished were fully reimbursed. The programs generated revenue that paid for the modernization of U.S. hospitals and the development of academic medical centers equipped with the most advanced technology.

universal health coverage. The U.S. economy was strong. Most leaders of the time accepted the idea that health care was a human right.

The Committee for National Health Insurance drafted a plan that would entitle all U.S. residents to health insurance under a federal insurance program. The plan would make Medicare and Medicaid unnecessary. Senator Edward M. Kennedy based his Health Security Act on this plan. Other leaders devised their own programs. By 1972, approximately 40 plans had been presented to Congress.

Conservatives backed plans that used tax credits to help people buy private health insurance. Liberals preferred public insurance plans that were supported by the federal government. These various plans became bogged down in discussions over how practical and effective they would be. Between 1972 and 1974 Nixon was caught up in the Watergate scandal. His resignation distracted from the debate. The ideal of universal health care lost its driving force.

In 1976, Jimmy Carter was elected president. He advanced a plan called Health Security. It was to be supported by employers and by an expansion of the Medicare and Medicaid programs. It also called for insurance holders to contribute large payments for their care. Senator Kennedy and Representative Henry Waxman developed a different plan—the Health Care for All Americans Act. Neither plan was adopted.

## From Reagan to Bush

From the 1980s to early 1990s, during the presidencies of Ronald Reagan and George H. W. Bush, political leaders were more concerned with containing health care costs than with expanding the system. In 1993, Bill Clinton revived the idea of universal health care. Health Security, which extended coverage to all, kept the existing hybrid structure. It relied on state funding and insurance provided by employers. It included new ideas on containing costs. However, this plan also failed.

Financial problems with Medicare and Medicaid became severe during the administration of President George W. Bush (2001–2009). Opponents of single-payer health care systems pointed to the problems of these two programs as evidence that socialized health care systems could not work.

Bush proposed several ways of helping people get affordable health care. In December 2003, he signed into law a new Medicare bill that included health savings accounts. These accounts made it possible for people to supplement their Medicare coverage with tax-free accounts for health care expenses not covered by Medicare. The bill also allowed taxpayers enrolled in high-deductible health plans to open health savings accounts.

Bush also recommended the creation of association health plans. These would permit associations of employers to purchase health insurance across state boundaries. The businesses in these associations could then pay lower premiums for better benefits. Bush then proposed several methods of reducing health costs. These included facilitating access to electronic medical records and limiting frivolous lawsuits against health providers. Bush also wanted to educate Americans to adopt healthy lifestyles and remove obstacles to putting cheaper, generic drugs on the market.

*President George W. Bush hosts a discussion
on health care initiatives in 2007.*

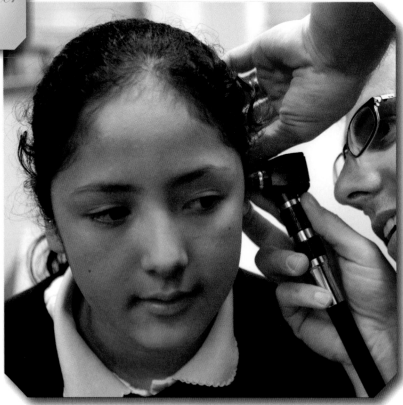

*Dr. Michael Paul examines a fourth grader in Illinois as part of the
Pediatric Mobile Health Unit of Loyola University Medical Center.*

# Is Health Care
# a Human Right?

he concept of human rights is rooted in
both religion and philosophy. Theologians
believe that humans have basic rights because they are
made in the image of God. Thomas Jefferson, the
main author of the Declaration of Independence,

based his claim that the colonists were entitled to rebel against Great Britain because "all men are created equal and endowed by their Creator with certain inalienable Rights—Life, Liberty, and the Pursuit of Happiness."[1] Jefferson's source for this idea was John Locke's *Second Treatise Concerning Civil Government*. In this book, Locke argued that governments exist to protect people's rights to life, liberty, and property. Locke and the American patriots influenced by him felt that reason, as well as religion, justify the idea of natural rights.

## Religious Justification

The idea that health care is a human right became prevalent during the early twentieth century. Reformers first began to consider ways to improve health care for the poor. John Ryan, a Catholic priest and professor of economics and ethics, wrote about the issue in *Living Wage: Its Ethical and Economic Aspects*. He argued that workers should be paid a "living wage" that would enable

### John Locke and Natural Rights

The *Columbia Encyclopedia* gives the following synopsis of John Locke's ideas on natural laws and the state: "Locke believed that the original state of nature was happy and characterized by reason and tolerance. In that state all people were equal and independent, and none had a right to harm another's 'life, health, liberty, or possessions.' The state was formed by social contract because in the state of nature each was his own judge, and there was no protection against those who lived outside the law of nature. The state should be guided by natural law."[2]

**The American
Red Cross's Efforts**

The American Red Cross is best known for offering medical and other services during and after disasters. It also has programs that teach ordinary people to help others. These services are described on the Red Cross Web site: "For nearly a century, the American Red Cross has prepared people to save lives through health and safety education and training. From first aid, CPR, and blood-borne pathogens training to swimming and life guarding, HIV/AIDS education, and Babysitter's Training, American Red Cross Preparedness programs help people lead safer and healthier lives."[4]

them to afford medical care. He asserted that health is a human need and, as such, a natural right. As a natural right, it must belong to all human beings, regardless of race, religion, or gender. Father Ryan felt that human rights have a divine origin. He argued, "The individual is endowed by nature, or rather, by God, with the rights that are requisite to a reasonable development of his personality."[3]

During the twentieth and twenty-first centuries, U.S. social reformers of most religious affiliations argued for universal health care. Catholic Church leaders, for example, have made the right to health care a doctrine. In addition to practicing the mission of healing, they have preached and written about health care and human rights issues. The 1981 pastoral letter "Health and Health Care" states:

> Every person has a basic right to adequate health care. This right flows from the sanctity of human life and the dignity

*that belongs to all human persons, who are made in the image of God.*[5]

## Health Care Is a Human Right

Many secular people also consider health care to be a human right. They believe that compassion, even if unrewarded by a divine being, must be shown toward fellow human beings. They also reason that meeting the needs of suffering people will reduce conflict in the long run and, therefore, lessen world misery.

To further its mission of promoting world peace, the United Nations (UN) has based many of its programs on that idea. It includes in its Universal Declaration of Human Rights the assertion, "Everyone has the right to a standard of living adequate for the health and well-being of oneself and one's family, including food, clothing, housing, and medical care."[6]

## Nongovernmental Organizations

Several nongovernmental organizations have embraced the UN's declaration and try to help people gain their human rights. Founded in France

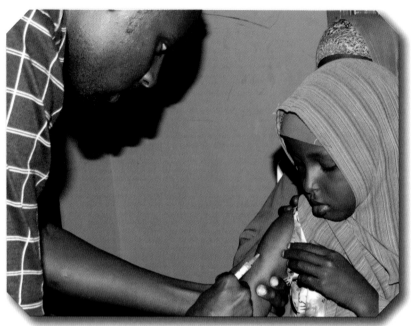

*A Somali child is vaccinated for measles at a Doctors Without Borders hospital in Somalia in 2007.*

in 1971, Doctors Without Borders is an organization especially concerned with people's health needs. It has expanded to an international movement. Doctors Without Borders has member groups in 19 countries, including the United States. All groups share the goal of bringing medical care to people whose lives have been disrupted by wars, epidemics, and natural disasters. Doctors Without Borders takes no sides in armed conflicts and gives aid to anyone who needs it. For its efforts to achieve a more peaceful world, the organization was awarded the Nobel Peace Prize in 1999.

## HEALTH CARE IS A NATURAL RIGHT

In the United States, many proponents of universal health care point out that the natural rights to life, liberty, and property include the right to health care as they do the right to be educated. Social worker Helen Redmond argues that, without a universal health care system, the possession of property is not possible for everyone. In the present system, she says, medical expenses are so high that sick people must often use all their resources to pay for them. If they cannot honor these expenses, they are in acute danger of bankruptcy.

The present health care system, Redmond says, threatens the freedom of the mentally ill. Insurance that covers mental illnesses is far inferior to insurance that covers physical illnesses. People who are psychotic are often unable to cope with the red tape of applying for Medicaid. Some end up living on the street. Delusional and panicked, they frequently cannot control their behavior and are locked up in prison—the ultimate loss of liberty.

## HEALTH CARE IS NOT A HUMAN RIGHT

Some opponents of a universal health care system contend there is no philosophical proof that people have a natural right to health care. Philip Barlow, consultant neurosurgeon at Southern General Hospital in Glasgow, Scotland, points out that the term "health care" is vague. In addition to covering basic measures such as immunization and treatment for diagnosed illnesses, it may include procedures such as cosmetic surgery and infertility treatment. Barlow feels that it must be made clear

### The Rights of Doctors

In 1971, Dr. Robert Sade wrote about the issue of rights for the *New England Journal of Medicine*. The article examined the question of whether health care is a human right from the physician's point of view:

> The concept of medical care as the patient's right is immoral because it denies the most fundamental of all rights, that of a man to his own life and the freedom of action to support it. Medical care is neither a right nor a privilege: it is a service that is provided by doctors and others to people who wish to purchase it. It is the provision of this service that a doctor depends upon for his livelihood, and is his means of supporting his own life. If the right to health care belongs to the patient, he starts out owning the services of a doctor without the necessity of either earning them or receiving them as a gift from the only man who has the right to give them: the doctor himself. . . . American medicine is now at the point in the story where the state has proclaimed the non-existent "right" to medical care as a fact of public policy, and has begun to pass the laws to enforce it.[7]

how extensive the medical care should be before demanding it as a human right.

He also states that the concept of human rights has no philosophical or practical basis. Human rights, he argues, are different from civil and political rights, such as a fair trial or the right to vote. These have the practical purpose of maintaining a free and stable society. Health care as a human right, on the other hand, is not politically feasible in countries with limited resources.

## The U.S. Government's Responsibility

Stephen Chapman is a writer of editorials on public issues. He explains why the U.S. government does not have to provide for health care as it does for civil rights, such as the right to a lawyer. Chapman argues that the government must help people accused of crimes to defend themselves because it is threatening them with imprisonment or execution. However, the government is not usually responsible for the illnesses that befall its citizens. Therefore, the government does not have to help them get better. The U.S. Constitution guarantees only that the government will protect the rights of its citizens, not provide for them.

Chapman goes on to say that obligating the government to provide health care for all U.S. citizens is actually a violation of civil rights. By forcing taxpayers to cover other people's medical costs, it "infringe[s] on the liberty and property of others."[8] The danger in identifying health care as a human right, he argues, is that this does not say what kind of care the government must provide. Does the responsibility extend to treating ear infections and rashes or to correcting perceived flaws in someone's appearance? This would drive up the cost of necessary treatment.

Most people who do not consider health care to be a human right agree on at least one point with those who do. They believe that the poor should have access to medical care. But if health care is categorized as something that everyone is entitled to have, the system that provides it will be overused and quickly drained of resources, opponents argue. They also fear that people will lose their self-reliance and let a central government gain too much control.

In 1998, President Clinton signed the Patient Bill of Rights, which outlined the rights and responsibilities for patients and health care providers.

*President George W. Bush's 2008 budget proposal included cuts to Medicare and Medicaid in an effort to balance the federal budget.*

# ECONOMICS OF NATIONAL HEALTH CARE

ocial critics point out that since the United States is the richest nation in the world, there is no excuse for 47 million Americans to lack health insurance. Some proponents of a single-payer system believe that it is the government's responsibility to make sure its citizens have effective medical care. A national health care system, they argue, would be more efficient and less expensive to run than the current hybrid system. Opponents of a single-payer system counter that it is not the government's responsibility to provide health care. They also contend that socialized health care would lead to more bureaucracy and greater expense. They feel that the system can only be improved by making it more market-driven than it is.

## CUTTING THE RED TAPE

Proponents of a single-payer health care system claim that one of the main problems with the hybrid U.S. system is that its complexity makes it too expensive. They point out that the more than 100,000 private health insurance carriers generate costly and time-consuming red tape. Clerical workers must be paid to prepare detailed bills, check and approve claims, verify that deductibles have been met, confirm that co-payments have been paid, and so forth.

Having one payer for health insurance, proponents argue, would eliminate the red tape that is clogging the U.S. health care system. The payer would be able to reduce clerical work substantially. Moreover, it would be able to control prices that are now set by powerful and profit-oriented groups such as insurance and pharmaceutical companies.

Steffie Woolhandler and David U. Himmelstein are professors of medicine at Harvard University. In their article, "Socialized Medicine: A Solution to the Cost Crisis in Health Care in the United States," they point out that national health insurance is not tied to market forces. Therefore,

### The Costs of a Single-payer System

John R. Battista, MD, and Justine McCabe, PhD, believe that a universal health care system would be cheaper than the current private health care system. They offer these reasons:

- The United States spends at least 40 percent more per capita on health care than any other industrialized country with universal health care.
- Federal studies by the Congressional Budget Office and the General Accounting Office show that single-payer universal health care would save $100 to $200 billion per year despite covering all the uninsured and increasing health care benefits.
- The costs of health care in Canada as a percentage of gross national product were identical to the United States when Canada changed to a single-payer, universal health care system in 1971. The costs have increased at a rate much lower than they have in the United States, despite the U.S. economy being much stronger than Canada's.
- Single-payer universal health care costs would be lower than the current U.S. system due to lower administrative costs.[1]

it would save money that medical businesses spend on advertising and other sales-related expenses. Woolhandler and Himmelstein also argue that the existing market system allows doctors to make too much money. Under single-payer systems in other countries, such as the United Kingdom, fee scales keep doctors' salaries in proportion to those of the rest of the population.

## MINIMAL BENEFITS

Americans spend an enormous amount on health care. Despite this, many people do not receive the medical services they need. The elderly and the very poor have access to Medicare and Medicaid. But patients who do not qualify for these programs must depend on charity. Other citizens end up paying for their care in the form of higher medical costs and taxes.

**Health Care Expenditures**

When it comes to health care, the United States spends far more per person than other industrialized countries. In its 2007/2008 Human Development Report, the United Nations listed the health expenditure per capita for each country. A sampling of the data includes:

- United States: $6,096
- Switzerland: $4,011
- Canada: $3,173
- Germany: $3,171
- France: $3,040
- United Kingdom: $2,560

Dr. Maria Dahl makes a house call to examine
an 87-year-old cancer patient in 2007.

People who buy their own insurance policies
have access to some of the best medical services in
the world. Few Americans can afford such policies,
however. Most insured Americans are covered
by policies provided to them by their employers.
Supporters of single-payer health care systems find
several problems with these job-related policies.
If employees leave their jobs, they cannot take the
policies with them. If their new employers provide
medical benefits, the new insurance companies

may refuse to cover medical costs
for preexisting health conditions.
Workers may move to smaller
companies that cannot afford to offer
health benefits.

Proponents of national health
insurance feel that patching up the
current hybrid system cannot bridge
the gap between the cost of the
system and the benefits it provides
for most U.S. citizens. They feel that
a single-payer system will not only
solve problems but also will cover
conditions, such as psychiatric care,
dental care, and prescription drug
costs, that Medicare and many private
insurance plans do not cover.

## THE PROBLEMS WITH GOVERNMENT INVOLVEMENT

Lin Zinser, JD, and Paul Hsieh,
MD, wrote the article "Moral Health
Care vs. 'Universal Health Care.'"
In it, they argue that the current
U.S. system is in financial trouble

**Efficient or Not?**

John Goodman is the founder and president of the National Center for Policy Analysis in Dallas, Texas. He disagrees that national health care would be more efficient than the present system: "We often hear that Medicare and Medicaid are efficient. The government says Medicaid only spends about two percent of its budget on administration. But that ignores all the costs that are shifted to doctors and hospitals. When you incorporate all those costs, it turns out that actually Medicare is not very efficient at all."[2]

## Emergency Care

The Emergency Medical Treatment and Active Labor Act of 1985 involves emergency care. It requires hospitals that accept Medicare patients to assess the condition of anyone who comes to the emergency room regardless of his or her ability to pay and regardless of whether he or she is insured. Opponents of government intervention in health care point out that this law robs the doctors forced to care for impoverished patients of payment for their services and prevents paying patients from getting the help they need in emergencies.

because it is already almost entirely nationalized. They point out that the federal government largely subsidizes job-related insurance polices. Both the employees who hold the policies and the employers that provide them enjoy large tax benefits.

To further support their case, Zinser and Hsieh discuss government-imposed mandates on health care. Benefit mandates, for example, determine the number and varieties of medical procedures that policies can cover, the types of health care providers that are included, and the types of health problems that will be reimbursed. These mandates make insurance more expensive than necessary, Zinser and Hsieh argue.

A mandate known as the "mandatory guaranteed issue" is particularly damaging to the nation's economy, according to Zinser and Hsieh. Under the mandatory guaranteed issue law, an insurance company in a given market must give policies to any group that applies. These

*The headquarters of Procter & Gamble, a large company that offers health insurance to its employees, are shown in Cincinnati, Ohio.*

policies must cover all members of that group. Small companies seeking to give good health plans to their employees benefit greatly from this mandate. Zinser and Hsieh argue that this wrongly diminishes the insurance companies' ability to make profits. To avoid losing money, insurance companies may charge larger premiums. In that case, poorer companies cannot offer health benefits to their workers.

## MEDICARE AND MEDICAID

Zinser and Hsieh believe that Medicare and Medicaid are too large a financial drain on the nation. The funding of these programs involves nearly 20 percent of the federal budget. Medicaid is managed by the states and takes up an average of 22 percent of their budgets. The authors state that because the federal government matches the money the states put into Medicaid, the states try to include too many people in the program. In some cases, they have granted membership to families with yearly incomes of $55,000.

Zinser and Hsieh believe many problems would be solved if all government controls were removed from the health care system. If that happened, they believe competition and other market-based regulations would bring down the costs of medical care and improve its quality.

*Many elderly individuals rely on Medicare for their prescription drugs.*

California Governor Arnold Schwarzenegger speaks about his health care reform proposal during a press conference in 2007.

# POLITICAL ASPECTS
## OF THE DEBATE

ertain issues have the power to split the U.S. population into opposing groups. Generally speaking, these groups fall into two different categories: liberal and conservative. Each group feels that its opinion best reflects the nation's ideals. How to reform the U.S. health care system is one of the issues that divide the public. People who support a socialized health care system tend to be liberals, while those who oppose it tend to be conservatives.

Politically liberal people tend to be concerned with social justice. Generally, they want the government to spend tax money on comprehensive social programs, such as health care and education. Conservatives tend to support less government intervention to preserve the freedom of U.S. citizens. They think that individual choice and free-market forces will have the best results in areas such as health care.

## LIBERAL VIEWPOINT

Proponents of socialized health care tend to be suspicious of the motives behind big business. As evidence, they point out that powerful groups in the medical

**Social Reform and the Structure of the U.S. Government**

In "Public Policies to Extend Health Care Coverage," E. Richard Brown explains why the United States has not achieved a universal health care system: "The United States has a very ingrained political culture that supports weak government, a tradition that goes back to the very founding of this country. The United States has never developed either a strong civil service or a tradition of people looking to government to solve social problems—a different set of popular expectations than prevail in other industrialized countries."[1]

industry have blocked reform for fear that it might threaten their own business interests.

In his article, "The Madness of the Market," Robert Sherrill discusses groups that he claims have exploited the U.S. health care system and that continue to resist changing a system that has enriched them. These groups include for-profit hospitals, doctors, drug companies, and insurance companies. He does not say that every member of each group robs the public. But he does feel that those members who do are so numerous that they have a significant impact on the health care system. He states that members of all these groups take advantage of their clients in the following ways:

❖ Doctors and hospitals order unnecessary procedures and overcharge for their services.

❖ Drug companies make misleading claims about the results of tax-funded research and tests done on their products.

❖ Drug companies use indirect bribes to persuade doctors to prescribe their medications.

❖ Insurance companies not only deny their policyholders life-preserving treatments, they

The logos of Blue Cross Blue Shield of Michigan, a health insurance provider, are seen on the company's headquarters in Detroit in 2008.

also sell fraudulent policies to such vulnerable groups as the elderly.

Sherrill states that these businesses have gained power for several reasons. Many people have a great trust in the medical profession. People fear becoming seriously ill and need to believe that, if they do, trustworthy professionals will be there to help. Sherrill also discusses ways in which medical business leaders have influenced the government. He says they use their great wealth to influence elections and to run advertising campaigns for and against government programs. Other national health advocates share Sherrill's attitude toward powerful industries. They warn that if the United States remains under their sway, it would end up with an inadequate health care system. It would also no longer be a democracy. Big businesses would run the government and enact legislation that benefits them at the expense of the rest of the population.

## Conservative Viewpoint

Many conservatives feel that the U.S. health care system should be in private hands. They believe that too much of the system already has been turned over to the government and that this is the source of its problems. Besides causing acute economic problems, they fear that socialized health care would decrease liberty in the United States.

In his article, "National Health Care and the Welfare State," Richard M. Ebeling states that a national system would turn into a bureaucracy powerless to deliver good health care. It also would decrease individual freedom and encourage corruption.

Ebeling describes the following scenario: United with the state, the insurance companies and medical institutions would find it easier than ever to set up monopolies. The health care budget would expand until the state would have to ration health care services. The government then would have to appoint boards to manage rationing and to determine who would be qualified to receive health care and the kinds of services they should get. The state then would have the power of life and death over its citizens. It also would control medical research and drug testing. This would limit,

## An Objection to the Kennedy-Griffiths Bill

In "The Political Fallacy That Medical Care Is a Right," Dr. Robert Sade discusses the Griffiths-Kennedy bill. The bill was proposed by Senator Edward Kennedy and Representative Martha Griffiths in 1971 as a plan for universal health care. Sade views it as a proposal for the kind of state control envisioned by Richard Ebeling. Sade points out that to facilitate the government's management of health care, the bill recommended an advisory board. Sade feels that, among other things, this board would take away the patient's ability to choose his or her own doctor. It would also take away the doctor's ability to choose his or her own course of continuing education. Additionally, it would prevent hospital administrators from deciding which staff members were best able to perform medical procedures.

Sade sums up his objections to the bill and to all other proposals of nationalized medicine: "The Kennedy-Griffiths bill is the closest we have yet come to the logical conclusion and inevitable consequence of two fundamental fallacies: that health care is a right, and that doctors and other health workers will function as efficiently serving as chattels of the state as they will living as sovereign human beings."[2]

if not destroy, scientific innovation and impartial
research choices. Ebeling envisions the formation of
a black market in medication and medical services as
people begin to seek ways of receiving proper care.
Choosing one's own health care then would be a
crime.

## Socialized Health Care's Effect on Individuals

Many conservatives are wary of big government.
Some think that large government-funded programs
encourage laziness and take away from people's
independence. Ebeling made this argument using
an example from history. He cites the following
statistics from 1880 to 1930 that indicate a decrease
in productivity among German workers:

> *In 1885, a year after socialized health insurance began, the
> average number of sick days taken by members of the system
> each year was 14.1. In 1900, the annual average number
> of sick days per member had gone up to 17.6; in 1925, it
> had increased to 24.4 days; and in 1930, it was an average
> of 29.9 days. People also were noticeably sicker around
> weekends and Christmas and New Year's Day.[3]*

According to Ebeling, government programs actually corrupt the morals of a society. While his may be an extreme view, many other conservatives are concerned about the effects of government involvement on individuals. They worry that government programs offering handouts would be subject to abuse, misuse, and waste. Socialized programs give too much power to government and make citizens dependent and passive.

## Considering Both Sides of the Question

Both liberals and conservatives want to preserve liberty in the United States. Many liberals believe that financial security, health care, and educational opportunity make it possible for people to live free and fulfilling lives. They support programs such as universal health care because they feel that everyone

### Is Health Care a Social Institution?

In *Our Unsystematic Health Care System*, Grace Budrys discusses whether health care systems are social institutions. Education, family, religion, the economy, and politics are all examples of social institutions. According to her, like these institutions, a health care system has the following characteristic: "It evolved to address a fundamental social need, and it was built on the same foundation as the other social institutions. The building blocks on which all social institutions are constructed comprise our basic cultural values, beliefs, traditions, and expectations about the behavior of others."[4]

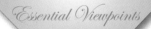

in society must have an opportunity to gain this liberating security. Some conservatives feel that a country can only be free if its citizens have strong, self-reliant characters. They look at such programs and ask, "How can a person who relies on government handouts be free?" They point out that the institutions on which people depend can use their dependence to control them. Liberals tend to feel that since a democratic government by definition consists of its citizenry, it cannot infringe on anyone's independence. After all, the citizens themselves will be managing the programs by choosing their administrators.

*Senator Hillary Clinton talks about health care reform while running in the Democratic presidential primary in 2007.*

Quebec Health Minister Philippe Couillard announces the new government policy on medication in Quebec City in 2007.

# THE CANADIAN HEALTH CARE SYSTEM

or proponents of socialized health care, Canada's system is a shining example. For opponents, it is a warning. Those in favor point out that Canadians spend less on their health care than Americans. Still, their infant mortality rate is

lower and their life expectancy is higher than that
of Americans. Opponents of socialized health care
point out that seriously ill people must wait for long
periods of time before receiving diagnostic tests and
treatment. They claim that Canadians pay large taxes
for slow, often inadequate, care.

## CANADA'S MEDICARE

Canada's government-funded health care system,
called Medicare, began functioning fully in 1962.
It is available to all permanent residents, regardless
of their incomes. Medicare covers care throughout
Canada and for medical emergencies incurred
during a temporary stay in another country.
Canada's provinces and territories manage their own
health care plans and pay for all necessary hospital
stays and doctors' services. In general, provinces
and territories have very similar plans that differ
mainly in their coverage of dental care, medical
prescriptions, optometric services, hearing aids,
and home care.

The federal government and the territorial and
provincial governments of Canada pay for Medicare
mainly with tax revenues. These include personal
and corporate income taxes and, in some provinces,

sales taxes. Also, in some provinces, people with higher incomes must pay special premiums. The federal government contributes approximately 40 percent of each province's health care plan if its plan meets federal standards.

As elsewhere in the world, the cost of health care in Canada is soaring. To better meet this increase in costs, some provinces have engaged in arrangements called private-public partnerships (P3s). In typical P3 arrangement, a medical facility is administered by a private company but paid for with public funds. Some Canadians

## A Brief History of Canada's Medicare

Grace Budrys gives the following account of how Canada's present health care system developed:

*In 1947, the province of Saskatchewan was the first to enact a provincial hospital insurance plan. In 1957, the federal government passed legislation establishing a national program to which the provinces would have to sign on and agreed to pay for half the costs. By 1961, all the provinces had adopted the plan. The financial windfall of federal support caused Saskatchewan to propose a new program to cover medical care costs (i.e., doctors' fees). The doctors did not like the hospital plan; however, they were vehemently opposed to the medical portion of the plan. They said that this was the beginning of socialized medicine, which would cause quality to decline, costs to go up because of mismanagement, and treatments to be determined by bureaucrats. The citizens of the province thought otherwise. Saskatchewan introduced medical insurance in 1961. The other provinces followed, and by 1971 Canada had a national health insurance program it called Medicare.[1]*

worry that the adoption of P3s eventually will lead to privatization of their health care system.

## Criticism of Canada's Medicare

Pierre Lemieux is an economist at the Department of Management Sciences of the Université du Québec in Outaouais, a research fellow at the Independent Institute, and a *Western Standard* columnist. In his article, "Socialized Medicine: the Canadian Experience," he expresses dissatisfaction with Canada's Medicare. He writes that to pay for this system, the government requires all residents to enroll in it. This means that, although people can buy extra insurance for such amenities as private or semiprivate hospital rooms, they cannot buy private insurance for basic care that is superior to what the public system offers.

Medicare pays fixed rates to its doctors. The doctors cannot charge their patients more than these rates. Canadian law permits doctors to leave Medicare and set up their own practices. But since people cannot buy private insurance to pay higher rates for basic care, most doctors do not do this. To increase their salaries, many doctors and other medical workers leave Canada to work in the United

States. As a result, Lemieux claims, Canada's health facilities tend to be understaffed. He also feels that the banning of private insurance policies affects the quality of health care in other ways. For example, it prevents the development of private hospitals. Lemieux believes that this gives the government a monopoly over Canada's health care system. It not only curbs the competition that leads to excellence but also limits the development of services not included in Medicare, such as home care.

**Unhealthy Delays**

In "Do We Want Social-ized Medicine?" Walter Williams states that a 2006 publication put out by the Fraser Institute gives the following information on the amount of time that patients have to wait from referral to treatment in the Canadian Medicare system: "The shortest wait-ing time was for oncology [cancer] (4.9 weeks). The longest waiting time was for orthopedic surgery (40.3 weeks), followed by plastic surgery (35.4 weeks) and neurosurgery (31.7 weeks)."[2]

## In Defense of Canada's Medicare

In *Our Unsystematic Health Care System*, Grace Budrys answers some of Lemieux's main objections to Canada's Medicare. Lemieux states that it is monopolistic for the government to control the entire system. Budrys responds that, being government run, Medicare is more democratic than the United States' hybrid system:

*The majority of Canadians like things just the way they are. The position of the majority is that, when everyone is in the same boat, that boat is likely to be much better cared for. In other words, it is always easier to deny funding to "them," but when it is "us" whose care is at stake, "we" tend to exhibit more concern and readiness to treat the topic of increased funding more seriously.[3]*

Budrys also points out that most Canadian doctors do not see government caps on their income as an intrusion. Provincial governments negotiate doctors' incomes with provincial medical societies that represent the doctors. She states that Canadian doctors consider the dictates of managed care and insurance companies to be more restrictive than government-imposed salary caps. Managed-care organizations and insurance companies not only limit the amount of money doctors can make, they interfere with their professional decisions by determining which procedures doctors can use.

Proponents point out that while Canada spends less on health care per person than the United States, Canadian citizens are healthier than Americans. Various studies have supported this claim. In 2006, *CIA World Fact Book* published statistics that showed Canada's infant mortality rates were lower than those in the United States and its life expectancy was longer. This was despite the fact that Canada's per capita spending on health care was approximately $3,000 while that of the United States was approximately $6,000.

## EFFORTS TO SOLVE CANADA'S MEDICARE PROBLEMS

Mark Grzeskowiak backs Budrys's assertion that Canadians tend to take responsibility for the performance of their health care system. In his article, "Health Care in Canada," he points out that groups such as the Canadian Health Care Association and the Canadian Nurses Association have focused on several of Medicare's biggest problems. These include:

❖ The amount of time patients must wait for important tests and treatment.

❖ Insufficient personnel and medical equipment.

**Waiting for Care**

Robert Evans and Noralou P. Roos defend their country's Medicare reputation in "What Is Right about the Canadian Health Care System?": "But what about the 'Canadian problem'—waiting lists? In the United States, people without money or insurance do not even get on a waiting list. Access is rationed by ability to pay, not by waiting. (They may gain access to care at some public facilities; but then they wait.)"[4]

*Canadian Prime Minister Paul Martin answers questions from the media about Canada's Medicare system.*

❖ The failure to fully cover home, pharmaceutical, and long-term care.

In 2004, the federal and provincial governments agreed to invest $41 billion (Canadian dollars) to solve some of these problems. To reduce waiting times, the government is using part of these funds to hire more personnel. Canada is also increasing the capacity of medical facilities and programs to serve more patients. Another portion of this money is being used to set up the Public Health Agency of Canada. In addition to searching for effective means of dealing with serious diseases and epidemics, the agency also is trying to improve access to health care in Canada's northern regions. Medical schools have been set up in these regions to encourage more doctors to practice there. The governments of the more northern provinces are working to improve communications within their areas. They have set up a service for people with health concerns to make free and confidential phone calls to registered nurses.

Proponents of Canada's system consider it a work in progress. They claim that with realistic appraisals of its problems, it can be a success. Opponents urge a return to a private system using the U.S. health care system as a model.

Roy Romanow, head of the Canadian Royal Commission on Health Care, discusses its report at a news conference in Ottawa, Ontario, in 2002.

*Pharmacist Jim Manning looks over prescription drugs on a shelf at Market Place Pharmacy in Minot, North Dakota, in 2006.*

# MEDICARE, MEDICAID, AND HMOS

Some of the most important measures taken to improve the U.S. health care system during the twentieth century were the institution of Medicare, Medicaid, and various managed-care plans. Medicare and Medicaid were intended to make access to health care more equal. Some conservatives believe that these plans are dangerously close to socialistic programs as they are mainly paid for and run by the U.S. government. The conservatives view managed health plans as less politically suspect since private groups run them.

## MEDICARE

Medicare is a federal program for the elderly. Qualification for membership depends on age, not on income. Members must be 65 years or older. The program is based on the assumption that, in general, elderly people have higher medical bills and smaller incomes than younger people. Medicare is considered an entitlement program. U.S. citizens are entitled to this insurance because they pay taxes for Social Security benefits that include Medicare.

Medicare has four parts. Part A pays for hospital stays, post-hospital skilled nursing facility stays, and

### Coverage for Low-income Children

The State Children's Health Insurance Program offers health coverage to low-income children under the age of 19. It was established as part of the Balanced Budget Act of 1997. Both state and federal governments fund the program. Each state has considerable freedom in the way it manages its program. All states, however, are required to provide the following services: inpatient, out-patient, and emergency treatment. They must also pay for well-baby and well-child visits as well as immunizations. Most states cover psychiatric care (including treatment for substance abuse).

home health care. Part B covers most basic doctor bills, laboratory fees, and some outpatient medical services. Part C entitles its enrollees to private managed care coverage as approved by Medicare. Part D pays some of the costs of prescription medications. All parts of Medicare require the patient to pay at least a small percentage of his or her medical costs.

## Medicaid

Medicaid is a program for low-income people of any age. The federal and the state governments support this program. Because the states help pay for the program, each state is free to manage it differently. Rules for the program vary from state to state. In some states, Medicaid requires all recipients to pay small amounts for some services.

In most states, Medicare recipients also can qualify for Medicaid, which may cover costs that Medicare does not. These may include prescription drug costs, diagnostic care, and eyeglasses.

## Financial Problems of Medicare and Medicaid

In 2007, more than 40 million U.S. citizens relied on Medicare for health care coverage. As life expectancy increases, the population includes a growing number of people vulnerable to the health problems of old age. Originally, it was predicted that the fund that pays for hospital and physician care would last until 2019. The entire Medicare program was predicted to continue until 2027. Even this less-than-optimistic prediction has become doubtful.

Julie Rovner, a health policy journalist, reported signs that Medicare funding might run out more quickly than anticipated:

### Urgent Problems

In 2008, *Fortune* senior editor-at-large Geoff Colvin wrote about the urgency of solving the problems of Medicare and Medicaid in "The $34 Trillion Problem." While politicians sometimes avoid this controversial issue, he explains why the nation's leaders need to start facing the realities:

*Sometime in the next president's first term, Medicare Part A (hospital insurance) will go cash-flow-negative. . . . Medicare provides a wide range of services and subsidies to more than 40 million old and disabled Americans. As the country ages, Medicare and Medicaid . . . will devour growing chunks of U.S. economic output. So will Social Security, but its cut of GDP [gross domestic product] should stop increasing about 2030. The federal budget has averaged about 18 percent of [gross domestic product] over the past several decades. If that average holds and if the rules of our social insurance programs don't change, then by 2070, when today's kids are retiring, Medicare, Medicaid, and Social Security will consume the entire federal budget, with Medicare taking by far the largest share.[1]*

*[This] warning is triggered when, for two years in a row, Part B—and other Medicare funding from general revenues—are expected to exceed 45 percent of total Medicare spending within seven years.*[2]

This trend was observed for the second year in a row in 2007. Medicaid also was in financial trouble. Medical costs had soared and a slumping economy had reduced tax revenues.

Another issue for Medicare and Medicaid was the need to balance the federal budget. The budget has been strained by the wars in Afghanistan and Iraq. In January 2008, President George W. Bush proposed cutting spending on Medicare by $6 billion in 2008. He also proposed a reduction of $91 billion from 2009 to 2013 by lowering payments to health care providers and increasing premiums for beneficiaries in higher income brackets. Bush also planned to initiate competitive bidding for Medicare lab services. Critics state the proposed cuts would have adverse effects on inpatient hospitals, outpatient hospitals, hospices, and ambulance services. Bush also wanted to cut spending on Medicaid by $1.2 billion in 2008 and approximately $14 billion over the next five years.

President George W. Bush gives a speech at the American Medical
Association's National Conference in 2003.

## Managed-care Plans

Managed-care plans are organizations designed
to decrease medical costs for their members.
The members pay an advance fee at a much lower
rate than if they paid for medical services as they
needed them. In 1938, industrialist Henry Kaiser
established a managed-care organization for
his employees. To encourage doctors to join his
organization, he assured them of an income. He
did this by requiring his workers to pay five cents

per day for medical care even if they never needed it. The workers had to go to one of the member doctors. As his company took on more projects, Kaiser organized more of these plans. They worked so well that he set up an organization separate from his building business. Its sole purpose was to provide his workers with health care insurance. He called it Kaiser Permanente. Gradually, other business leaders set up similar health care plans. All of these early organizations were nonprofit.

The managed-health organizations that developed from the Kaiser Permanente model are largely for-profit businesses. The best known of these are the Health Maintenance Organizations (HMOs). An HMO consists of a network of doctors who have contracted to work for the organization for an amount of money set by the organization. When clients enroll in an HMO, they pay a fixed fee, called a premium. The premium entitles clients to medical care from any doctor in the HMO network.

In 1974, President Richard Nixon was alarmed at the financial problems of Medicare and Medicaid. He endorsed managed-care plans as a possible solution. To encourage their growth, Nixon persuaded Congress to pass a bill requiring business

*House Republicans Phil Gingrey and John Boozman talk about the Medicare Part D prescription drug plan in 2006.*

owners to include these organizations as an option in their employee benefits packages. The bill also allotted funds to help people establish new HMOs.

## OBJECTIONS TO HMOs

With these economic incentives, more businesspeople began to set up their own HMOs. As they did so, fewer of the organizations were run on a nonprofit basis. The business leaders who ran them looked for ways to cut costs to make profits.

Soon people began to criticize HMO leaders for making medical decisions that were based more on their own financial benefit than on the health of their clients. Many people also disliked having their choice of health care providers limited to the doctors in the HMO network.

HMOs are not the only prepaid health care plans. Clients of point-of-service plans can go to doctors outside their plan's network if they pay an extra fee when they do so. Preferred provider organizations have a selected list of doctors from which their clients can choose. These cost a little more money than other prepaid plans.

At first, the various attempts to improve the state of the U.S. health care system showed promise. They brought down insurance prices and increased access to medical care. However, their advantages were soon outweighed by the rapid and steep rise in health care costs and by inappropriate management of health care organizations.

### In Defense of HMOs

Physician and cancer patient David Jacobsen defends Health Maintenance Organizations: "I do not doubt that HMOs, like any other business, sometimes serve their customers poorly. But there is no reason to believe that managed care systematically undermines patient welfare because of the imperative to cut costs. To the contrary, I have found that efficiency is perfectly compatible with compassionate, effective health care. . . . I [am] myself . . . a cancer patient. Thus far, my care has been unsurpassed. I have the option of being treated outside my HMO, but would not think of going anywhere else."[3]

Demonstrators rally to support Medicaid funding outside
the state capitol in Santa Fe, New Mexico, in 2008.

*Renate Pore, right, listens to speakers at a health reform rally as part of a Cover the Uninsured Week event in West Virginia in 2008.*

# MANDATORY
# HEALTH INSURANCE

*S*ome health care reformers believe that universal coverage and improved health care can be achieved without converting to a single-payer system. One possible way of doing this is to require everyone by law to have a health insurance policy. It may be bought by an individual or provided by the employer. Reformers acknowledge that the policies must be affordable. And subsidies must exist for people who cannot pay as much as others for policies. If these conditions were met, they assert that a mandatory health insurance system would solve many economic and health problems.

Michael E. Porter and Elizabeth Olmsted Teisberg coauthored *Redefining Health Care: Creating Value-Based Competition on Results*. They discuss the advantages of mandatory health insurance. They make proposals on how to shape it into a workable system in a free-market economy. The authors point out that an entire society is affected financially when some of its members become ill or disabled. Therefore, because everyone is vulnerable to health problems, everyone must pay a share of the costs. They argue that besides being fair, distributing the cost among an entire population would make each person's payment smaller.

## Uninsured

Porter and Teisberg cite surveys showing that many people who can afford to buy policies often do not do so. These people tend to be young and

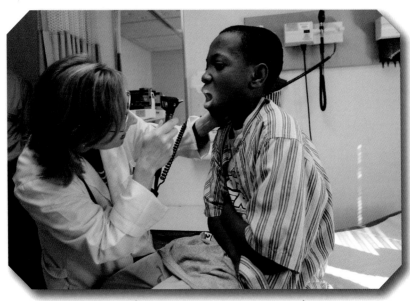

*Dr. Maura Shea examines a patient in Massachusetts, where health care coverage is now mandatory.*

confident that their good health will continue. When people refuse to buy insurance plans, it places a burden on others. It means that premiums will be higher for those who do buy health insurance. When uninsured people develop health problems and seek treatment, they must pay for the care out of pocket. Medical bills not paid in part by insurance are often so high that even people with comfortable means cannot meet them. Often, uninsured people put off treatment or seek medical help from emergency rooms.

## Affordable Health Insurance

Porter and Teisberg believe that national mandatory health insurance provides a practical way to prevent drains on public health funds. Although means to help the poor should be available, the government should not automatically cover all their expenses. The authors suggest that vouchers based on income should be distributed to poor people. They could use them to buy insurance at lower prices. Another option would be to enroll poor people in Medicaid and require them to pay premiums based on their incomes.

## Preventing Fraud and Discrimination

Another challenge is to prevent people who can afford private health coverage from taking advantage of subsidies for the poor. Porter and Teisberg say that records of income should be checked more thoroughly. Under the current system, they claim, it is possible for people to qualify for subsidized health care by falsifying their financial records.

The authors also state that mandatory insurance would help high-risk people. This includes people who have trouble buying insurance because they have chronic health conditions. Each state could distribute the number of such cases among various insurance plans. Several companies would share the cost of their care and keep the clients' premiums low.

Porter and Teisberg have proposed several other measures to make insurance more affordable and accessible for everyone. They suggest limiting insurance coverage to essential, basic care and making sure that all employers provide their employees with insurance plans. They also advise preventing insurance companies from imposing unfair or unreasonable rules on their clients. Porter and Teisberg also suggest that insurance companies should be required to take full responsibility for medical bills.

## CASE STUDY: HAWAII'S MANDATORY INSURANCE SYSTEM

Some states that are trying to institute universal care systems are considering mandatory health insurance. For the past 34 years, Hawaii has had a mandatory health care system. It has not yet achieved universal coverage.

In 1974, Hawaii's government passed the Prepaid Health Care Act. The law was to be managed by Hawaii's Department of Labor and Industrial

Relations. The requirements took effect on
January 1, 1975. All employers in that state had
to offer health
insurance to
employees who had
worked 20 or more
hours per week for
four consecutive
weeks.

Under this law,
all plans must be
equal in benefits
to the Hawaiian
insurance plan
that has the
greatest number
of members.
Each plan covers
standard hospital
care, surgical
procedures
(including after-
care visits),
diagnostic
laboratory services,

**An Objection to Mandatory Insurance**

Claudia Chaufan teaches health policy and
sociology of health and medicine at the University of California at Santa Cruz. Chaufan
believes that the argument for mandatory health
insurance is based on a shaky foundation:

*A key assumption underlying individ-
ual mandates is that forcing an influx of
"customers" into the health insurance
marketplace, flooded with private insurers' "products" made to suit a range of
personal preferences will . . . improve
the quality of medical goods and services
and bring their prices down, such that on
average they will be affordable to every-
body. . . . A mandate to buy, for instance,
drivers' insurance, does not guarantee full
protection against the expenses incurred if
one gets into a car accident. While some
policies might cover those expenses, they
are unlikely to be cheap. What the current
mandate to buy drivers' insurance "guarantees" . . . is that, given the law, we won't
get in trouble with it if we are stopped by
the police. . . . Likewise, whichever health
insurance policies we may afford to buy
. . . it will only "guarantee," aside from a
steady pool of clients for private insurers,
that we are in compliance with the law
when we file our taxes.[1]*

and maternity benefits. Employers must continue to pay their share of a disabled worker's premium for three months after the person becomes disabled and is unable to work. Disabled workers also must pay their share.

A 2004 report gives the following explanation of how employer and employee share the cost of health insurance:

> Hawaii employers may cover the full cost of the health insurance premium, or share the cost with their employees. Based on a fixed formula, the law requires employers to contribute 50 percent of the premium cost of single coverage, and the employee must contribute the balance, as long as the employee's share does not exceed 1.5 percent of his or her wages.

> A person who works 40 hours per week at a salary of $10 an hour would earn $1,733 per month. If the cost of

### Cost Savings

Representative John M. Mizuno supports the goal of universal health care in Hawaii:

"If Hawaii has access to the best health care in the country, why is the Legislature even considering universal health care for all residents? The answer is simple: cost savings. By providing health care to Hawaii residents through a single-payer system, employers, hospitals, and the state will save money. Late-stage emergency care will be reduced for those who cannot afford medical care."[2]

*insurance (single coverage) is $150 per month, half that
amount is $75, and 1.5 percent of the worker's salary is
$26. As stipulated by the Act, the worker would pay the
lesser of the two amounts ($26) and the employer pays the
rest ($124).[3]*

## HAWAIIANS WHO ARE NOT COVERED

Not every working Hawaiian is insured. The
following groups are excluded from the mandate:
government workers, seasonal workers, people
who work for commissions (such as insurance
agents and real estate agents), and those who are
self-employed. Some people have no jobs and,
therefore, no insurance. Many Hawaiians feel that
mandatory health insurance can be the answer
to bridging the gap between the insured and the
uninsured. They point to the fact that, a year after
mandatory insurance was imposed, the percentage
of the uninsured dropped from 30 percent to
approximately 5 percent. Unfortunately, this
percentage has increased. In 2003, the number of
uninsured was estimated at 10 percent. To decrease
this percentage, many organizations are funding
efforts by the Hawaii Uninsured Project to extend

health coverage to all Hawaiian residents.

## MASSACHUSETTS FOLLOWS HAWAII'S LEAD

In 2006, Massachusetts passed a law requiring health care coverage for all residents. To enforce this mandate, the government imposed a $295 tax on each business owner who did not provide employees with health insurance. In 2008, the state had not yet achieved universal coverage. Nonetheless, the effects of the law seemed encouraging. Since 2006, more than two-thirds of the state's uninsured had obtained some type of coverage. Other states watched to see if the plan's promise will be fulfilled. ⁓

"In the end, we need to make health care more affordable for Americans without sacrificing efficiency, quality, and innovation—the great price we pay for big-government medicine. We shouldn't force insurance on our citizens; we should try instead to fix insurance. All states, including Hawaii, should deregulate restrictive insurance laws and encourage more personal freedom of choice in consumer-directed health plans. Once insurance is more affordable, people will enroll voluntarily."[4]
—Diana M. Ernst, health care policy fellow at the Pacific Research Institute

*Jeremy Eden earns too much money to qualify for Medicaid but too little to buy insurance. He would benefit from mandatory health insurance.*

*Barack Obama talks about health care during a discussion at the Ohio State University Medical Center in Columbus, Ohio, in 2008.*

# THE LATEST PLANS FOR
# IMPROVEMENT

*I*n 2008, the U.S. health care system's two main problems—unequal access to health insurance and the rising costs of medical treatment—still remained unresolved. Some reformers wanted to introduce socialized health care similar to Canada's

system. Others wanted to reduce the government's
role in health care. Still others wanted to repair
the existing system without radically changing it.
The issue was prominent in the 2008 presidential
election, which Senator Barack Obama won over
Senator John McCain. Health care reform was an
important item in their campaign platforms. Each
favored building on the existing multipayer system
but had a very different vision of what such a system
should do and how it could do it.

## PRESIDENT OBAMA'S HEALTH PLAN

Obama believed that access to health care
should be universal. During his 2008 campaign,
he asserted that this could be accomplished without
eliminating the current private insurance system.
He suggested that the U.S. health system should
include competing private insurance companies
and one government program similar to Medicare.
To coordinate and monitor private insurance plan
transactions, he supported the creation of a National
Health Insurance Exchange. This agency would
help all individuals and small businesses to obtain
affordable private insurance. The government would
provide subsidies based on income for those unable

to pay the standard insurance rates. With some exceptions, all employers would have to contribute to insurance coverage for their employees. All plans purchased under the National Health Insurance Exchange would give coverage comparable to the health benefits that federal employees and members of the U.S. Congress receive.

Other features of Obama's plan included portability (policyholders could keep their plans even if they left their jobs) and accessibility (no one could

### John McCain's Health Plan

Republican presidential candidate John McCain did not support a single-payer system. However, he believed that health care should be more accessible. He wanted to lower the cost of insurance by increasing competition among insurance companies. Under his plan, individuals still would have the option of obtaining insurance through their employers. But tax credits would be available to purchase private insurance if they wanted. Not only would people find health insurance more affordable, they would be better able to choose a plan that suited their needs, McCain argued. Like President George W. Bush, McCain believed that people should be encouraged to build their own health savings accounts.

McCain also planned to work with state governments to develop a guaranteed access plan. The plan would help people with preexisting health conditions to obtain health insurance. McCain suggested a nonprofit organization that would make it possible for insurance companies to join with companies in other states. These companies would share the expenses of covering clients with preexisting conditions.

McCain's plan also aimed to lower prescription drug costs, treat chronic conditions more efficiently, and tighten regulations on various health care agencies and providers.

be denied insurance because of a preexisting health condition). This plan would have two mandates. All parents would be required to insure their children. And all employers who did not insure their workers would have to give part of their payroll to the government insurance program.

## Cutting Health Care Costs

Catastrophic illnesses and injuries are those that have a devastating and long-term effect on a person's life. They include severe burns, amputations, neurological disorders, and other serious conditions. One reason that health insurance premiums are so high is that these types of health issues are expensive to treat. Obama proposed that the government reimburse employer health plans for a part of these expenses. In return, the employee's premiums would be reduced.

"We now face an opportunity—and an obligation—to turn the page on the failed politics of yesterday's health care debates. . . . My plan begins by covering every American. If you already have health insurance, the only thing that will change for you under this plan is the amount of money you will spend on premiums. That will be less. If you are one of the 45 million Americans who don't have health insurance, you will have it after this plan becomes law. No one will be turned away because of a preexisting condition or illness."[1]
—*President Barack Obama*

John McCain talks to doctors, nurses, scientists, and health care workers in Tampa, Florida, in 2008.

Under Obama's plan, the government would support disease management programs. These would improve quality of care and lower costs of treating such chronic conditions as diabetes and high blood pressure.

The National Health Insurance Exchange, as envisioned by Obama, would regulate and monitor hospitals and health providers. It would ensure that their reports about quality and costs were complete and accurate.

## The Debate over Health Care Reform

Many people were dissatisfied by the plans proposed by Obama and McCain. Proponents of a single-payer health care system felt that the multipayer systems supported by both candidates were inefficient and liable to corruption. They feared that, as treatments for the wounded U.S. health care system, these plans would be no more effective than a Band-Aid.

The debate over health care reform has raised important questions—some ideological, some practical. Among these are:

❖ Is health care a human right that the U.S. government is obligated to provide?

❖ Would governmental control of the health care system threaten individual freedom?

### Objections to Obama's Proposal

One person who saw problems with Barack Obama's plan was Paul Krugman. He criticized Obama's plan for not mandating coverage. Krugman wrote about it in the *New York Times*: "Under the Obama plan, healthy people could choose not to buy insurance, then sign up for it if they developed health problems later. This would lead to higher premiums for everyone else. It would reward the irresponsible, while punishing those who did the right thing and bought insurance while they were healthy."[2]

❖ Which system, national or private, would give better access to quality health care?

❖ Which system, national or private, would most effectively reduce the rising costs of health care?

The well-being of the U.S. economy and population depends to a large extent on the answers to these questions. Perhaps the nation's pressing need will inspire Americans to work together to find these answers. ⌒

Mary White, from Marianna, Florida, takes part in a health care rally in 2006, in Tallahassee, Florida.

# TIMELINE

| 1884 | 1916 | 1935 |
|------|------|------|
| Chancellor Otto von Bismarck nationalizes health care in Germany. | The American Association of Labor Legislation proposes that health insurance be supported by state taxes. | Franklin D. Roosevelt signs the Social Security Act into law. |

| 1961 | 1965 | 1971 |
|------|------|------|
| All Canadian provinces adopt the country's Medicare system. | Lyndon B. Johnson signs Medicare and Medicaid into law. | The Kennedy-Griffiths Bill is unsuccessfully proposed. |

| 1938 | 1945 | 1948 |
|---|---|---|
| Henry Kaiser establishes a managed-care organization for his workers. | Harry S. Truman proposes his Federal Health Insurance Plan to Congress. | The United Nations General Assembly adopts the Universal Declaration of Human Rights. |

| 1971 | 1973 | 1975 |
|---|---|---|
| Doctors Without Borders is founded in France. | The Health Maintenance Organization Bill is passed. | Hawaii's Prepaid Health Care Act goes into effect. |

# TIMELINE

| 1979 | 1981 | 1985 |
|------|------|------|
| Jimmy Carter unsuccessfully proposes his plan for universal health coverage, Health Security, for the second time. | The American Catholic Bishops issue the pastoral letter "Health and Health Care." | The Emergency Medical Treatment and Active Labor Act becomes law. |

| 2007 | 2007 |
|------|------|
| Total U.S. health care costs increase to $2.3 trillion. | More than 40 million Americans rely on Medicare for health coverage. |

| 1993 | 2003 | 2006 |
|------|------|------|
| The Clinton Health Security Act is presented to Congress. It is never enacted into law. | George W. Bush signs a new Medicare bill into law that includes health savings accounts. | Massachusetts passes its Mandatory Health Insurance Program Act. |

| 2007 | 2007 | 2008 |
|------|------|------|
| Michael Moore's movie *Sicko* is released. | Forty-seven million Americans have no health insurance. | George W. Bush proposes major cuts to Medicare and Medicaid. |

# ESSENTIAL FACTS

## AT ISSUE

### Opposed to a Single-payer System

❖ Health care is not a human right. The government is not obligated to provide it.

❖ A national health care system would be less efficient than a private system.

❖ A national health care system will not make health care more accessible.

❖ A national health care system would increase taxes.

❖ A national health care system lacking a profit incentive would lower the quality of health care.

### In Favor of a Single-payer System

❖ Health care is a human right that the government should provide.

❖ A national health care system would be more efficient than the current U.S. health care system.

❖ A national health care system would ensure equality of health services.

❖ A national health care system would be less expensive than the current hybrid health care system.

❖ A national health care system would improve the quality of health care.

## CRITICAL DATES

### August 14, 1935
Franklin D. Roosevelt signed the Social Security Act into law.

### July 28, 1965
Lyndon B. Johnson signed Medicare and Medicaid into law.

### 1973
The Health Maintenance Organization Bill was passed.

**January 1, 1975**
Hawaii's Prepaid Health Care Act went into effect.

**1985**
The Emergency Medical Treatment and Active Labor Act became law.

**December 1, 2003**
George W. Bush signed a new Medicare bill into law that included health savings accounts.

**April 2006**
Massachusetts passed its Mandatory Health Insurance Program Act.

## QUOTES

"We share a common goal: making health care more affordable and accessible for all Americans. The best way to achieve that goal is by expanding consumer choice, not government control."—*George W. Bush*

"The quality of health care in the United States has deteriorated under for-profit, managed care, and treatments should not be designed based on a corporation's quest to save money. While saving money may make a company's stock go up, denying health care to the sick is immoral."—*John Mugarian*

# ADDITIONAL RESOURCES

## SELECT BIBLIOGRAPHY

Anderson, Ronald M., Thomas H. Rice, and Gerald F. Kominski, eds. *Changing the U.S. Health Care System: Key Issues in Health Services, Policy, and Management.* San Francisco: Jossey-Bass, 2001.

Budrys, Grace. *Our Unsystematic Health Care System, Second Edition.* Lanham, MD: Rowman & Littlefield Publishers, 2005.

Derickson, Alan. *Health Security for All.* Baltimore, MD: The Johns Hopkins University Press, 2005.

Himmelstein, David U., and Steffie Woolhandler. "Socialized Medicine: A Solution to the Cost Crisis in Health Care in the United States." *Why the United States Does Not Have a National Health Program.* Amityville, NY: Baywood Publishing Company, 1992.

Opdycke, Sandra. *No One Was Turned Away: the Role of Public Hospitals in New York City.* New York: Oxford University Press, 1999.

Porter, Michael E., and Elizabeth Olmsted Teisberg. *Redefining Health Care: Creating Value-Based Competition on Results.* Boston, MA: Harvard Business School Press, 2006.

Sherrill, Robert. "The Madness of the Market." *The Nation.* January 1995: 45–72.

## FURTHER READING

Grover, Ian, ed. *Current Controversies: Health Care.* Farmington Hills, MI: Greenhaven, 2007.

Haugen, David M. *Opposing Viewpoints: Health Care.* Farmington Hills, MI: Greenhaven, 2008.

Marcovitz, Hal. *Health Care.* Broomall, PA: Mason Crest, 2006.

## Web Links

To learn more about health care reform, visit ABDO Publishing Company online at **www.abdopublishing.com**. Web sites about health care reform are featured on our Book Links page. These links are routinely monitored and updated to provide the most current information available.

## For More Information

For more information on this subject, contact or visit the following organizations.

**American Medical Association**
515 North State Street, Chicago, IL 60610
800-621-8335
www.ama-assn.org
The American Medical Association is a professional association of U.S. physicians. It distributes information about important medical matters to its members and to the general public.

**American Society of Law, Medicine, and Ethics**
765 Commonwealth Avenue, Suite 1634, Boston, MA 02215
617-262-4990
www.aslme.org
The American Society of Law, Medicine, and Ethics offers educational opportunities for people in the medical profession and is a source of information on a variety of health care topics and issues. Its extensive library contains books on law, medicine, ethics, and health care.

**Heritage Foundation**
214 Massachusetts Avenue Northeast, Washington DC 20002
www.heritage.org
This institute publishes information on the conservative stance on a variety of topics. It researches methods of changing the current U.S. health care system to one based on consumer choice and free-market competition.

# Glossary

**bankruptcy**
The state of being judged legally to be unable to pay off debts.

**bureaucracy**
Complex rules and regulations applied rigidly.

**capitalistic**
Related to an economic system based on the private ownership of the means of production and distribution of goods, characterized by a free competitive market and motivation by profit.

**epidemic**
An outbreak of a disease that spreads more quickly and more extensively among a group of people than normally would be expected.

**federal**
Relating to a central government.

**fraudulent**
Relating to the crime of obtaining money or some other benefit by deliberate deception.

**hybrid**
Something made up of a mixture of different elements.

**inflation**
A continuing increase in the general price levels.

**insurance**
Purchased protection against medical expenses or other losses.

**legislation**
The process of writing and passing laws; laws passed by an official body.

**mandatory**
Needing to be done, followed, or complied with, usually because of being officially required.

**monopoly**
A situation in which one company controls an industry or is the only provider of a product or service.

**mortality**
The number of deaths in a given time.

**nationalize**
To transfer a business, property, or industry from private to governmental control or ownership.

**pharmaceutical**
Involved in or associated with the manufacturing, preparation, dispensing, or sale of the drugs used in medicine.

**premium**
The sum of money paid, usually at regular intervals, for an insurance policy.

**privatization**
The change from public to private control of ownership.

**ration**
To restrict the amount of something that an individual is allowed to buy, consume, or use.

**revenue**
The income of a government from all sources.

**single-payer**
A system in which health care services are paid for by the government instead of individuals.

**socialism**
A political theory or system in which the means of production and distribution are controlled by the people and operated according to equity and fairness rather than market principles.

**subsidize**
To contribute money to somebody or something, especially in the form of a government grant to a private company, organization, or charity.

**universal**
Available to all members of society.

# SOURCE NOTES

**Chapter 1. Evaluating the U.S. Health Care System**
1. John Mugarian. "Capitalism in Health Care Does Not Work."
*The Journal*. 13 July 2007. 28 July 2008 <http://www.johnmugarian.
com/2007/07/capitalism_in_health care_does.html>.
2. Edward Kennedy. "Remarks of Senator Edward M. Kennedy
on Health Care." 28 Apr. 2002. *John F. Kennedy Presidential
Library & Museum*. 28 July 2008 <http://www.jfklibrary.org/
Historical+Resources/Archives/Reference+Desk/Speeches/EMK/
Remarks+of+Senator+Edward+M.+Kennedy+on+Health+Care.
htm>.
3. George W. Bush. "State of the Union Address." 28 Jan. 2008.
*The White House*. 28 July 2008 <http://www.whitehouse.gov/infocus/
health care>.

**Chapter 2. Overview of U.S. Health Care Reform**
1. Sandra Opdycke. *No One Was Turned Away: The Role of Public Hospitals in
New York City since 1900*. New York: Oxford University Press, 1999.
21–22.
2. Larry DeWitt. "The Medicare Program as a Capstone to the
Great Society—Recent Revelations in the LBJ White House Tapes."
May 2003. *A Miscellanny of History, Philosophy and Public Policy*. 28 July
2008 <http://www.larrydewitt.net/Essays/MedicareDaddy.htm>.

**Chapter 3. Is Health Care a Human Right?**
1. Thomas Jefferson. "The Declaration of Independence."
*Independence Hall Association in Philadelphia*. 4 July 1776. 28 July 2008
<http://www.ushistory.org/Declaration/document/index.htm>.
2. "John Locke." *The Columbia Encyclopedia, Sixth Edition, 2001-2007*. 28
July 2008 <http://www.bartleby.com/65/lo/Locke-Jo.html>.
3. Alan Derickson. *Health Security for All: Dreams of Universal Health Care
in America*. Baltimore, MD: The Johns Hopkins University Press,
2005. 6.
4. American Red Cross. "Health and Safety Services." <http://www.
redcross.org/SERVICES/hss>.
5. "United States Conference of Catholic Bishops Preamble."
*Faithful Reform in Health Care*. 28 July 2008 <http://www.
faithfulreform.org/index.php/Theology-and-Policy/United-
States-Conference-of-Catholic-Bishops.html>.

6. "Universal Declaration of Human Rights." *United Nations*. 10 Dec. 1948. 28 July 2008 <http://www.un.org/Overview/rights.htm>.
7. Robert Sade, MD. "The Political Fallacy That Medical Care Is a Right." *New England Journal of Medicine*. Association of American Physicians and Surgeons. 2 Dec. 1971. 28 July 2008 <http://www.aapsonline.org/brochures/sademcr.htm>.
8. Stephen Chapman. "Medical Care Is Not a Human Right." *Health Care and Human Values: Ideas in Conflict*. Hudson, WI: Gary E. McCuen Publications, 1993. 37.

**Chapter 4. Economics of National Health Care**
1. John Battista and Justine McCabe. "The Case for Single Payer, Universal Health Care for the United States." *Connecticut Coalition for Universal Health Care*. 4 June 1999. 28 July 2008 <http://cthealth.server101.com/the_case_for_universal_health_care_in_the_united_states.htm>.
2. John Goodman. "Five Myths of Socialized Medicine." *Cato's Letter*. 2005. 28 July 2008 <http://www.scribd.com/doc/2341873/CATO-Five-Myths-of-Socialized-Medicine-John-Goodman>.

**Chapter 5. Political Aspects of the Debate**
1. E. Richard Brown. "Public Policies to Extend Health Care Coverage." *Changing the U.S. Health Care System: Key Issues in Health Services, Policy, and Management*. Eds. Ronald M. Andersen, Thomas H. Rice, Gerald F. Kominski. San Francisco: Jossey-Bass, 2001. 51.
2. Robert Sade. "The Political Fallacy that Medical Care Is a Right." *New England Journal of Medicine*. Association of American Physicians and Surgeons. 2 Dec. 1971. 28 July 2008 <http://www.aapsonline.org/brochures/sademcr.htm>.
3. Richard M. Ebeling. "National Health Insurance and the Welfare State." *Freedom Daily*. Feb. 1994. 28 July 2008 <http://www.fff.org/freedom/0294b.asp>.
4. Grace Budrys. *Our Unsystematic Health Care System*. New York: Rowman & Littlefield Publishers, 2005. 3.

## Source Notes Continued

**Chapter 6. The Canadian Health Care System**

1. Grace Budrys. *Our Unsystematic Health Care System*. New York: Rowman & Littlefield Publishers, 2005. 147–148.

2. Walter Williams. "Do We Want Socialized Medicine?" *Capitalism Magazine*. 15 Aug. 2004. 28 July 2008 <http://www.capmag.com/article.asp?ID=4924>.

3. Grace Budrys. *Our Unsystematic Health Care System*. New York: Rowman & Littlefield Publishers, 2005. 148.

4. Robert Evans and Noralou P. Roos. "What Is Right about the Canadian Health Care System?" *Physicians for National Health Plan. Third World Traveler*. Mar. 2000. 28 July 2008 <http://www.thirdworldtraveler.com/Health/WhatsRight_CanadaHC.html>.

**Chapter 7. Medicare, Medicaid, and HMOs**

1. Geoff Colvin. "The $34 Trillion Problem." *Fortune. CNNMoney.com*. 24 Mar. 2008. 28 July 2008 <http://money.cnn.com/2008/03/03/news/economy/104239768.fortune/index.htm>.

2. Julie Rovner. "Medicare Money Problems Trigger Warning." *National Public Radio*. 24 Apr. 2007. 29 July 2008 <http://www.npr.org/templates/story/story.php?storyId=9794068>.

3. David Jacobsen. "Cost-Conscious Care: In praise of HMOs." *Reasononline*. June 1996. 28 July 2008 <http://www.reason.com/news/show/29946.html>.

**Chapter 8. Mandatory Health Insurance**
1. Claudia Chaufan. "What's Wrong with Individual Health Insurance Mandates?" *The Health Care Blog*. 29 Feb. 2008. 29 July 2008 <http://www.thehealth careblog.com/the_health_care_blog/2008/02/index.html>.
2. John H. Mizuno. "Is Hawaii Ready for Universal Health Care?" *Hawaii Business*. Feb. 2008. 28 July 2008 <http://www.hawaiibusiness.com/Hawaii-Business/February-2008/Spin-Zone/>.
3. "Hawaii's Prepaid Health Care Act Ensures Health Coverage for Some Workers." *The Hawaii Uninsured Project*. 29 July 2008 <http://healthcoveragehawaii.org/pdf/PrepaidHealthCareAct.pdf>.
4. Diana M. Ernst. "Hawaii and the Quest for Universal Health Insurance." *Grassroot Institute of Hawaii*. 8 Aug. 2007. 29 July 2008 <http://www.grassrootinstitute.org/GrassrootPerspective/UniversalHealthQuest.shtml>.

**Chapter 9. The Latest Plans for Improvement**
1. Barack Obama. Speech. Iowa City, IA. 29 May 2007. *Obama '08*. 29 July 2008 <http://www.barackobama.com/issues/healthcare/#lower-costs>.
2. Paul Krugman. "Obama's Health Care Plan: The Mandate Muddle." *New York Times*. 7 Dec. 2007. 29 July 2008 <http://www.commondreams.org/archive/2007/12/07/5687/>.

# INDEX

# ABOUT THE AUTHOR

Lillian E. Forman is a former high school English teacher who now writes and edits educational materials for students. Forman says that what she loves most about her new profession is the opportunity to learn about a wide variety of topics. Forman has also published short stories for children. For her own pleasure, she writes personal essays and poetry.

# PHOTO CREDITS

Christine Balderas/iStock Photo, cover; Justin Sullivan/Getty Images, 6; John Bazemore/AP Images, 12; Mike Derer/AP Images, 15; AP Images, 16, 22, 45; Charles Dharapak/AP Images, 27; Tim Boyle/Getty Images, 28; Mohamed Sheikh Nor/AP Images, 32; Ruth Fremson/AP Images, 37; Scott J. Ferrell/Congressional Quarterly/Getty Images, 38, 75; Rusty Kennedy/AP Images, 42; Bill Zimmer/AP Images, 47; Max Whittaker/AP Images, 48; Carlos Osorio/AP Images, 51; J. Scott Applewhite/AP Images, 57; Jacques Boissinot/AP Images, 58; Tom Hanson/AP Images, 65; Fred Chartrand/AP Images, 67; Jill Schramm/AP Images, 68; Rick Bowmer/AP Images, 73; Natalie Guillen/AP Images, 77; Bob Bird/AP Images, 78; Joe Raedle/Getty Images, 80; Charlie Riedel/AP Images, 87; Rick Bowmer/AP Images, 88; Steve Nesius//AP Images, 92; Phil Coale/AP Images, 95